093118

Welsh

It's Wales

Quiz Book

Jim Green

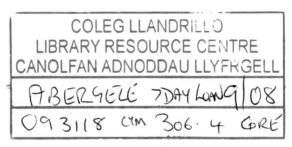
Cover design: Elwyn Ioan

ISBN: 0 86243 720 2

Printed on acid-free and partly recycled paper
and published and bound in Wales by
Y Lolfa Cyf., Talybont, Ceredigion SY24 5AP
e-mail ylolfa@ylolfa.com
website www.ylolfa.com
tel (01970) 832 304
fax 832 782

Contents

Introduction

What makes quiz games like Trivial Pursuits, or pub quizzes or TV quiz games or quiz books like this one so fascinating? I don't know. Maybe it's because they give people a chance to show off their general or specialist knowledge, or maybe it's because if you don't know the answer you learn something when you find out what the correct answer is. Maybe it's a form of education you can enjoy because it's quite painless (unless the people you play with are information snobs) and you can enjoy it wherever and whenever you like among people you like being with. Who knows – who cares? So long as you and others enjoy themselves.

This quiz book is full of fascinating questions (and answers) about Wales, the Welsh, their history, people, language, sport, arts and artists and anything else I could think of. Wales is the perfect country to provide quiz questions, it's got just about everything – famous places and people, mystery and history, crimes and religion, old and new, good and bad – like I say, just about everything.

So, enough introduction, let's get on with the questions and – pob lwc!

'That's Not the Right Answer!'

The curse of quizzes, whether in pubs or among family or friends, is the person who says, 'That's not the right answer. The right answer is...' and then gives a different answer from the one everyone's just been given. Needless to say the right answer is always the one they had given and been told is wrong. What can I say about the questions and answers in this book? Are they OK? That is, do the questions all come with the right answers? I have to say that despite my best efforts to use authoritative and reliable sources I can't be absolutely 100% certain. The problem is that Wales is something of an enigma; its very name illustrates that enigma. The name 'Wales' may be derived from a Saxon word meaning, roughly, 'foreigner' or 'outsider', whereas the name the Welsh have for their country, Cymru, means 'friend' or 'companion' – these opposites live comfortably alongside each other meaning the same thing for the purposes of day-to-day use. The questions in this quiz are questions I have asked myself about Wales and things Welsh and the answers I provide are the most accurate I have been able to find from the best authorities available. I don't think it would help for me to quote all the sources I have used because there are so very many authoritative Welsh sources and they don't always agree. Wales works in its own way and, if you're Welsh, you probably know that and can live with the fact that one right answer isn't necessarily the only right answer for many of the questions that can be asked about Wales. If you're not Welsh you'll just have to accept that Wales is not England or Scotland or Ireland or anywhere else; animated discussion and passionate disagreement are often par for the course for just about anything, from poetry to parrots. Anyway, here are about 500 questions and answers on Wales and things Welsh. If any of the answers I have provided are inaccurate or a truly better answer exists then please let me know via the publishers, and I'll try to see that a correction is made in any new editions.

Places

Wales is not a big country if you measure it simply by its surface area. But it would be difficult to think of any other place of similar size which has so much of interest packed into it. The castles and shrines, the odd and the marvellous, national parks and spectacular coastlines, the good, the bad and the ugly – they're all there and a lot more.

1. Which is recorded as the wettest settlement in Wales since modern records began?
    a) Aberystwyth
    b) Bala
    c) Capel Curig
    d) Crickhowell
    e) Holyhead

2. Which Welsh town has been host to those two truly great events; the World Bog Snorkelling Championships and the Mid Wales' Beer Festival?
    a) Builth Wells
    b) Llandeilo
    c) Llandovery
    d) Llandrindod Wells
    e) Llanwrtyd Wells

3. When Wales was made up of the old counties, which was Wales' smallest county in size?

4. Name the three national capitals closest to St. David's in Pembrokeshire in order of nearness.

5. Wales has always been a land of churches, chapels and holy places. In what year was St. John's established as Brecon's Cathedral?
    a) 932
    b) 1293
    c) 1329
    d) 1923
    e) 1932

6. Which of the following has the highest proportion of people under 16?
    a) Blaenau (Gwent)
    b) Flintshire
    c) Merthyr Tydfil
    d) Newport (Gwent)
    e) Pembroke

7. The Heart of Wales railway line is one of the most beautiful railway journeys in Britain. Where are its two terminus stations?
a) Cardiff	b) Liverpool
c) Swansea	d) Chester
e) Newport	f) Abergavenny
g) Hereford	h) Aberystwyth
i) Shrewsbury	

8.   What is the short name for The National Mining Museum of Wales?

9.   Welsh place names are often little word pictures. Which of the following place names, in English, means 'The church of David in the valley of the little river Honddu?'
      a) Dewi Fawr
      b) Llanddewi Brefi
      c) Llangynidr
      d) Llanthony
      e) Nantgaredig

10.   Llywelyn Fawr (Llywelyn the Great, died 1240) had a hound, Gelert, which guarded his infant son's cradle and killed a wolf thereby saving the child's life. Llywelyn saw the blood, jumped to the wrong conclusion, and slew the hound. The dog's grave is in the village of Beddgelert. When was it erected?
      a) 1236
      b) 1240
      c) 1800
      d) 1940
      e) 2000

11.   Strata Florida was one of Wales' many medieval monasteries, situated on a remote site in west mid-Wales. It was famous for a secret, sacred relic kept there. What relic was kept there?
      a) Joseph of Arimathea's staff
      b) Mary's veil
      c) the Holy Grail
      d) a piece of the true Cross
      e) the head of the spear that pierced Christ

12. Welsh is widely spoken and very much alive as a language. Where in Wales was the first secondary school established which used Welsh as the language of instruction?
    a) Aberystwyth
    b) Argentina
    c) Caernarfon
    d) Oswestry
    e) Rhyl

13. Which Welsh town returned the first ever Labour Member to Parliament?
    a) Llandudno
    b) Merthyr Tydfil
    c) Neath
    d) Pontypool
    e) Swansea

14. What does the name Llanbedr Pont Steffan (Lampeter) mean in English?
    a) the place of lambs
    b) church in the valley
    c) the village of lights
    d) the church of Peter by the bridge of Stephen
    e) east lambs field

15. At Frongoch, near Bala, there closed in 1894 the last production site in a long line which died out due to the intolerance of the Temperance movement in Wales. What did they make at Frongoch?

16. Which mountain is home to the sources of the rivers Severn and Wye?

17. Wales can reasonably claim to have one of the holiest burial sites in the Christian world. Where would you go to find the burial site of 20,000 saints?
    a) Bardsey Island
    b) Barry Island
    c) Llandaf Cathedral
    d) St. David's
    e) Swansea

18. Which river reaches Cardigan Bay at the town of Cardigan?

19. Which is Wales' biggest natural lake?

20. Which pilgrimage site in Wales has the longest unbroken history of Christian pilgrimage in the United Kingdom?
    a) Bardsey Island
    b) Caldey Island
    c) Holywell
    d) St. Beuno's Well
    e) Valle Crucis Abbey

21. Welsh history has often been very violent and castles are a feature of the Welsh landscape. Which is Wales' oldest substantially surviving stone built castle?
    a) Chepstow
    b) Conway
    c) Harlech
    d) Pembroke
    e) Rhuddlan

22. What is the name of the road bridge which joins Anglesey to the mainland?

23. Who designed it?

24. King Offa tried to keep out the wild Welsh by building a great rampart. It didn't work, of course, but it still exists today. Which two towns are at the ends of Offa's Dyke?
    a) Chester
    b) Newport (Gwent)
    c) Shrewsbury
    d) Rhyl
    e) Chepstow
    f) Wrexham
    g) Flint
    h) Prestatyn
    i) Hereford
    j) Monmouth

25. What modern business was first begun in Newport (Powys) by Pryce Pryce-Jones in 1859?
    a) mail order shopping
    b) bicycle manufacture
    c) screen printing
    d) post card printing
    e) wood laminating

26. Which mountain is named after a Welshman born in Breconshire?
    a) Ben Nevis (Scot.)
    b) Mount Everest (Nepal–Tibet)
    c) Mount Barrington (NSW Aus.)
    d) Mount Rushmore (USA)
    e) Mount Whitney (USA)

27. Which Welsh island is today home to a functioning Christian monastery?
    a) Anglesey
    b) Bardsey Island
    c) Caldey Island
    d) Ramsey Island
    e) Skomer Island

28. Wales may have its own Royal Prince today but where was Owain Glyndŵr declared King of Wales by a free Welsh parliament in 1404?
    a) Cardiff
    b) Chester
    c) Harlech
    d) Llandaf
    e) Machynlleth

29. The Welsh have always got about a bit across the world. The Welshman Elihu Yale went to America and became the major benefactor among the founders of Yale University. Where is he buried?
    a) Llandaf Cathedral
    b) Llandudno Municipal Cemetery
    c) St. Patrick's Cathedral, New York
    d) St. David's Cathedral
    e) Wrexham Parish Church

30. Welsh Spa Towns became very popular in Victorian times attracting thousands of visitors via the new railways. Which was the biggest of the Welsh spas?
    a) Builth Wells
    b) Llandrindod Wells
    c) Llanwrtyd Wells

31. T. E. Lawrence, famous as Lawrence of Arabia, was born in which part of Wales?
    a) the Brecon Beacons
    b) the Llŷn Peninsula
    c) the North Wales Coast
    d) the Vale of Neath
    e) the South Wales mining valleys

32. The odd but popular tourist village of Portmeirion, made famous by the equally odd TV series, 'The Prisoner', was designed to be like Portofino in Italy. In what year was building begun?
    a) 1794
    b) 1888
    c) 1903
    d) 1926
    e) 1947

33. Wales is a small country but it is home to the largest what in Europe?
    a) tree
    b) chapel
    c) car park
    d) Roman burial site
    e) bog

34. Which small Welsh town has decided to call itself 'the second-hand bookshop capital of the world' and hosts a big annual literary festival?

35. A copy of the oldest book in the Welsh language, written by medieval monks, is now in the National Library of Wales. Its snappy title is 'The Black Book of...' what?
    a) Carmarthen
    b) the Devil
    c) St. David
    d) Sin
    e) Wales

36. Where was a land speed record of 146 mph set by Sir Malcom Campbell in 1926?

37. The poet and drinker Dylan Thomas lived in and is buried in the village of Laugharne on the coast south west of Carmarthen. Did he live in...
    a) the boat house
    b) the pub

c) his wife's parents' house

d) the harbour master's house

e) a fisherman's cottage

38. Where was Prince Charles invested as Prince of Wales in 1969?

39. Wales is a land well endowed with water. In which modern county is Wales's highest waterfall?

a) Clwyd

b) Dyfed

c) Gwent

d) Gwynedd

e) Powys

40. Which of these towns is home to the National Library of Wales?

a) Aberystwyth

b) Bangor

c) Cardiff

d) Denbigh

e) Lampeter

41. The present title of Prince of Wales was an import from England. The first time it was conferred was on the son of that naughty and very violent English king, Edward 1st. Where did it take place?

a) Caernarfon

b) Chester

c) Edinburgh

d) Lincoln

e) London

42. Edward I was a great castle builder. Which was the last of his castles to be built in Wales?
    a) Beaumaris
    b) Conwy
    c) Cricieth
    d) Flint
    e) Pembroke

43. Many-towered Conwy castle has, unusually for a medieval fortress, a four-towered suspension bridge approaching it across the Conway estuary. When was it added to the castle?
    a) 1726
    b) 1826
    c) 1896
    d) 1906
    e) 1926

44. You can walk Offa's Dyke border fortification quite safely today. It is now designated as a long-distance footpath which was opened in July 1971. How many miles long is it?
    a) 86m
    b) 106m
    c) 136m
    d) 168m
    e) 186m

45. Aberdaron is a little village at the tip of the Lleyn Peninsula in North Wales. In the village is a popular café which still has the ancient name, Gegin Fawr. What does the name mean in English?

a) big kitchen
b) big house
c) big barn
d) big hole
e) big chimney

46. Bethesda in Gwynedd was once the home of the biggest what in the world?
   a) non-conformist chapel
   b) slate quarry
   c) donkey sanctuary
   d) working men's institute
   e) toilets built by public subscription

47. Which of the following has the highest ratio of men to women?
   a) Anglesey
   b) Bridgend
   c) Flintshire
   d) Monmouth
   e) Powys

48. The A5 has been a main road into and out of North Wales since Roman times. If you leave Wales by this road today what is the last Welsh town you would pass through?
   a) Chirk
   b) Corwen
   c) Gobowen
   d) Llangollen
   e) Ruabon

49. Put these places in order of size by population.
    a) Cardiff
    b) Holyhead
    c) Newport (Gwent)
    d) Swansea
    e) Wrexham

50. In 1801 Wales had a population of about ½ million. Which was Wales' most populous place at that time?
    a) Cardiff
    b) Llangollen
    c) Merthyr Tydfil
    d) Newtown (Powys)
    e) Wrexham

51. How long do you think the Welsh coastline is, to the nearest 50 miles?

52. Betws-y-Coed is a well-known beauty spot and tourist attraction. What does the name mean in English?
    a) glen of the faeries
    b) falls among the forest
    c) air and water
    d) chapel in the wood
    e) place of the birds

53. Which place in Wales has the highest rainfall?

54. Is it possible to travel entirely within Wales by rail from Llandudno on the north coast to Llanelli on the south coast?

55. Wales is not a big country. But how many miles would you say it was from top to bottom, to the nearest 10 miles?
    a) 90m
    b) 130m
    c) 170m
    d) 200m
    e) 210m

56. How much of Wales is given over to agriculture (to the nearest 10%)?

57. The Welsh have got just about everywhere in the known world at one time or another. So where would you think the settlement of Cwm Hyfryd was established?
    a) Argentina
    b) British Columbia
    c) New South Wales
    d) Scotland
    e) Wales

58. OK, so Wales isn't big by international standards. But what do you think is the area of Wales, to the nearest 1000 sq. km?

59. Wales is home to Northern Europe's smallest medieval Gothic cathedral. Where is it?
    a) Bangor
    b) Llandaf
    c) St. Asaph
    d) St. David
    e) St. Woolos

60.   Everyone knows that Snowdon is Wales' highest mountain, but just how high is it, to the nearest 100 feet?

61.   At which engagement did the 24th Regiment of Foot (soon afterwards re-named the South Wales Borderers) fight an action in which the highest numbers of VC medals given in a single action were awarded?

62.   What was Chepstow racecourse converted to in 1939?
        a) an assembly camp for enemy aliens awaiting internment
        b) an aircraft runway and maintenance facility
        c) temporary stabling for the Royal Horse Artillery
        d) temporary HQ of the Welsh Home Guard
        e) a barrage balloon storage facility

63.   Which Welsh port – one of the finest natural harbours in Europe – has been a home to Norwegian and Irish pirates, Dutch refugees, Georgian traders, a fishing fleet, was a chief embarkation point for Ireland and is still today one of Wales' main ports?

64.   Newport (Gwent) was for many years an important sea port. On which river was the port built?

65.   What is the modern name for Isca Silurium which was home to the Roman 2nd Augustan Legion from around AD70–140?

66.   Cardiff sits on which river?

67. Which town boasts a castle with the most elaborate defence system of any medieval fortress in Britain, and its own cheese?

68. Which river estuary provides the northernmost border between Wales and England?

69. Everyone knows that Snowdon is Wales' highest mountain, but which is Wales' second highest peak?
    a) Cader Idris
    b) Carnedd Dafydd
    c) Carnedd Llewelyn
    d) Glyder Fawr
    e) Tryfan

70. Which seaside town is terminus to the Ffestiniog Light Railway?

71. What did the Marquis of Bute present to the people of Cardiff in 1947?
    a) public park
    b) castle
    c) library
    d) public toilets
    e) collection of paintings

72. Which of the old Welsh counties had the largest area?

73. Which river finally reaches the sea at Rhyl?

74. Which river valley is regarded as providing the unofficial boundary between North and South Wales?

75. Where does England's second city, Birmingham, get most of its water from?

76. What part of Wales picked up the odd description, 'Little England beyond Wales'?

77. What is the English name for Y Trallwng, the county town of Montgomeryshire?

78. Wales' second city, Swansea, stands on which river?

79. Name the three National Parks of Wales.

80. Which of the old Welsh counties was supposed to be the most sparsely inhabited and the poorest, giving rise to the local saying, 'never a park and never a deer and never a squire for five hundred year'?
    a) Cardiganshire
    b) Denbighshire
    c) Flintshire
    d) Pembrokeshire
    e) Radnorshire

81. The Mumbles and the Worm's Head are at either end of which part of Wales?

82. The great Welsh hero and leader Owain Glyndŵr is commemorated in a modern long-distance footpath from Knighton to Welshpool. When was it opened in its present form?

    a) 1975
    b) 1986
    c) 1998
    d) 2000
    e) 2002

Sport

With a population of just around 3,000,000 you would think that Wales wouldn't be much of a player on the stage of world sport – but you'd be wrong. Wales has, over the years, produced far more than its fair share of top men and women in sport. Of course you may not always spot this, because Wales, along with Scotland, suffers from TV commentators' habit of pointing out that 'the Welshman came fifth' or 'that's another win for a British athlete'. But in golf, snooker, athletics, football, rugby, and a host of other sports, Wales has shown that it can provide competitors fit to take on the world.

1. Welsh ace Kelly Morgan won a US Open in 2003. What was her sport?
   a) badminton
   b) bowls
   c) golf
   d) judo
   e) pursuit cycling

2. Newport (Gwent) became home to a new National Stadium in 2004. What sport does it host?
   a) bowls
   b) cycling
   c) indoor athletics
   d) indoor tennis
   e) swimming

3. The great Tony Allcock retired from bowls in 2003 with a record number of titles under his belt. How many?
   a) 8
   b) 12
   c) 15
   d) 21
   e) 35

4. Llandaf North pulled off the coveted Welsh national 'treble' in 2003. What was their sport?
   a) bowls
   b) cricket
   c) cycling
   d) rugby
   e) tennis

5. Poor old Ivor Lloyd lost a title he had held for 20 years in 2003. What's more, he lost it to a woman who knocked 27 minutes off his time. What were they competing at?
   a) cycling
   b) rowing
   c) sailing
   d) skiing
   e) walking

6. When was the Welsh Racing Drivers Association founded?
   a) 1910
   b) 1931
   c) 1956
   d) 1981
   e) 2001

7. Eric Burden represented Wales at European and World level 11 times between 1988 and 1999. What was his sport?

8. The Welsh wizard Mary Ann Richardson showed she was the best Compound Lady in the Euronations Open Event of 2001 whilst Mal Whitter scooped third Compound Gent place for Wales in the same tournament. What was their sport?

9. How many years separated the establishment of the Welsh Men's Athletics Championships from the establishment of the Welsh Women's Championships?
   a) 0 (founded the same year)
   b) 10 years
   c) 19 years
   d) 26 years
   e) 59 years

10. What sport in Wales finally got a suitable venue when it took over an abandoned chicken farm on what had once been an airfield near Llanelli?

11. The whizzing Welshman Colin Jackson set a Welsh National Outdoor record for the 100m of 10.29 secs in July 1990. Where did it happen?
    a) Auckland
    b) Brussels
    c) Lausanne
    d) Tallin
    e) Wrexham

12. In what sport is a Welsh club side ranked in a higher division than the Welsh side?

13. Sandra Greatbach served Wales at international level 12 times between 1990 and 2002. What was her sport?
    a) archery
    b) bowls
    c) darts
    d) fishing
    e) motor racing

14. Which sport hosted the Celtic Super Prix?
    a) athletics
    b) cycling
    c) fly-fishing
    d) motor racing
    e) power boat racing

15. The Welsh darts legend Leighton Rees pulled off a wonderful 'treble' when he was in the Welsh team that won the World Cup Championships, the World Cup Team Champions and he won the World Cup Singles title. What was the year?
    a) 1969
    b) 1972
    c) 1977
    d) 1981
    e) 1985

16. Welsh wonder Nicole Cooke became the youngest-ever winner of a World Cup Series in 2003. In what sport did she achieve this?
    a) cycling
    b) mountain-biking
    c) rowing
    d) sailing
    e) snow-boarding

17. In 1977 Welshman Tom Pryce was killed while competing in South Africa. What was his sport?
    a) athletics
    b) climbing
    c) motor racing
    d) motor cycling
    e) mountain biking

18. What year was the Welsh Cricket Association founded?
    a) 1884
    b) 1913
    c) 1948
    d) 1969
    e) 1982

19. Angela Tooby set Welsh National Records in 3 athletic track events between 1987–88. What were her distances?

20. Julian Winn of Abergavenny became the first Welsh winner of a British Championship in 2002 which led him to a place with Team Fakta in 2003 and a go on the 'Giro'. What's his sport?

21.   Where did Gary Sobers make 36 off one over in August 1968?

22.   What was the year Woosie Wowed the Masters?

23.   1958 was a weird year for Welsh football. They were drawn from the group of European runners-up to give a game to a national team who couldn't get matches. They won the match which meant they went to the finals in Sweden. Who did they beat to get to the finals?

24.   Who was Cliff Thorburn playing when he made his televised 147 in a second round match at the Crucible in the 1983 World Snooker Championship?

25.   Which Welshman subbed for Andy Adams on Party Politics and for Tom Henks on Earth Summit to score two Grand National wins?

26.   Panic Attack from Torfaen was a winner at what in 1999?

27.   What year did Colin Jackson hurdle to a World Championship title in Stuttgart?
    a) 1990
    b) 1991
    c) 1992
    d) 1993
    e) 1994

28.   Juventus paid a world record fee of £65,000 to get John Charles in 1957. Which club got the cash?

29.   Gareth Edwards made 53 consecutive appearances for Wales at
        rugby. How many were as captain?
        a) 5
        b) 9
        c) 11
        d) 13
        e) 20

30.   Where was Celtic and Wales striker John Hartson born?
        a) Cardiff
        b) Llandudno
        c) Neath
        d) Swansea
        e) Wrexham

31.   Ynystawe village team visited Lord's in London to play in which
        final?

32.   Wales scored a surprise victory over New Zealand in 2002 to
        pick up a World Rugby Championship title. What was special
        about this Welsh team?

33.   Which Welsh football team, formed in 1873, which plays at
        the Racecourse Ground, has two nicknames, the Robins and
        the Red Dragons?

34.   Which Welsh National Team was formed in July 2001 and lost
        their first game to Alberta B but beat England 4–1 in May
        2002?

35. Robert Croft, the England Test spinner, was born in Swansea. What county team did he play for when he got his first Test call-up?

36. What sport is a regular feature at Bangor on Dee?

37. A poll of 800 Welsh women in Swansea, carried out in 2003, found that 82% thought Welsh rugby players had sexier what than their English counterparts?

38. What year did Terry Griffiths lift the World Snooker Crown?

39. Who upset Arsenal on April 23rd 1927 at Wembley?

40. What year did Lyn Davies leap to Olympic Gold?
    a) 1960
    b) 1964
    c) 1968
    d) 1972
    e) 1976

41. What was Ray Reardon's job before he became a snooker wizard?

42. What was brought to Wales for the third time after a victory at Taunton in 1997?

43. For an entry fee of £100 Sirrell Griffiths decided to have a go at what and found himself a winner at 100–1?

44. Tommy Farr went the distance in 1937. Who kept him company?

45. When was the Football Association of Wales founded?
    a) 1876
    b) 1896
    c) 1901
    d) 1905
    e) 1913

46. The Last Suspect managed to keep Hywel Davies on board for two laps to land a victory in what in 1985?

47. Who was the Welsh Football Team's manager for 47 days in 1994 and saw them lose to Norway?

48. The dapper and extrovert 'Lord of Brighton' lost to Joe Calzaghe in 1997. Joe went on to pick up a World title, enabling him to join the Welsh Hall of Fame in which sport?

49. Wales scooped Gold, Silver and Bronze with New Zealand only managing 5th and 6th places in which Open event in 1997?
    a) coracle racing
    b) fly-fishing
    c) sheep shearing
    d) speed knitting
    e) three-legged racing.

50. Katherine Huxley captained a Welsh National side that beat Devon and took on Middlesex. What's the sport?

51. What Welsh U-19 National Team beat England, Scotland and Canada before jetting off to the US for the World Championships?

     a) archery

     b) judo

     c) lacrosse

     d) snow boarding

     e) women's football.

52. What sport finally found a home in Wales at Tenby in 1888?

53. Howard Winstone picked up an Empire Games Gold, a British title and a world championship in which sport?

54. The Welsh Amateur Swimming Association was founded in:
    a) 1897
    b) 1923
    c) 1948
    d) 1956
    e) 1975

55. Which Welsh Sports Governing Body states on its official web site that 'Roller', 'Street', 'Rink', 'Underwater' and 'Ice' are not forms of the sport it deals with?

56. When the 'Sloth' met the 'Grinder' they stuck at it from 9pm to 3.50am the next morning. What were they doing?

57. They began with a goalless draw at Hartlepool, got through 3 managers, conceded over 100 goals, got relegated from the football league and set the worst league record in history in the 1987–88 season. Who were they?

58. When the almost all-conquering Kiwis made their 1963–64 tour of the UK they only lost one match. Who beat them?

59. What did Hugh Johns do in 1966 that no-one remembers?

60. How many times did Wales scoop the UK Amateur Golf Championship during the 1980s?

61. Richard Jones won an Interbrew sponsored Welsh Championship at the Dolphin Hotel in Swansea in 2003. What was the sport?

62. Georgio Chinaglia was a top Italian footballer before becoming president of the Italian club Lazio. Where did Georgio begin his professional football career?

63. Jonathan Jones is a 4 times World Champion at which sport?
    a) archery
    b) crazy golf
    c) dominoes
    d) mountain biking
    e) power boat racing.

64. Which top Welsh player won the Benson and Hedges Masters and got to the final of the Embassy World Championships in 2000?

65. This event was inaugurated in 1922 but a Welshman never got into the UK and Ireland side until J. Llewellyn Jones who played in the 1951, 1953 and 1955 sides. What is the event?

66. David Broome represented Britain at an amazing 6 Olympics. What was his sport?

67. Janet Ackland became the 1ˢᵗ Welsh Champion in 1988 at which sport?
    a) bowls
    b) dry slope skiing
    c) roller-blading
    d) snow-boarding
    e) women's wrestling

68. The Millennium Stadium in Cardiff had the biggest what in the world when it opened?

69. When Llangollen hosted the British Open Championships in 2002 what did the competitors sit in?

70. A Glamorgan man invented a golf scoring system which is named after him. What is it?

71. Which Welsh jump jockey took up thriller-writing when his days in the saddle were over?

72. The Dudson Valve (needle type) was named after its Welsh inventor and became a vital sports accessory. What was it?

73. Tanni Grey-Thompson broke over 20 world records and gruelled it out to win in London five times between 1992 and 2001. What's her sport?

74. Agnes Davies (nee Morris) picked up her first title, Welsh Ladies Champion in 1937 and managed the finals of the Welsh Regal Ladies over 40s in 2003 as well as picking up a couple of bowls titles. What was she good at?

75. Carwyn James, player and coach, is credited by some as the creator of the 'get your retaliation in first' school of which sport?

76. Which racecourse hosts the Welsh Grand National?

Sport can be a funny old business in many ways. How do you get to represent your country, for instance? Do you have to be born there, live there, have relatives there? And, if so, would a second cousin twice removed or a great aunt on your mother's side count? In the next five questions, name the well-known sporting personalities who have either claimed Welsh qualifications or had them claimed (however tenuously) for them.

77. An F.A. Cup Winner, premier league player for several clubs, Welsh international who captained the side against Holland. He finally gave up kicking a football to become a star of the big screen. His gran and granddad were from Bala. Who is he?

78. Born in Tunbridge Wells, this cricketer played for Leicester and captained England. He made 18 test centuries before becoming a radio and TV personality. It is said that he is a descendant of a Welsh Dowager Duchess who was the 1899 UK Croquet Champion and lived in Castell Malgwyn in Cardiganshire. Who is he?

79. When Wales beat England at cricket by eight wickets and 57 runs at Sophia Gardens, Cardiff in 2002 there was a 'Welshman-for-a-day' in their winning side. His normal international identity is a South African all-rounder and he had played for Western Province and Middlesex but as he was, at the time, a Glamorgan player he joined the Welsh team and the rest is history. Who is he?

80. This top golfer was a bit of an international mix. He was born on March 17th, St. Patrick's Day, and learnt his trade by following and copying local Scottish pro Stewart Maiden. He won his first tournament at the age of six, and won his first invitation tournament aged 13 in Birmingham, Alabama, in his home state of Georgia. He won 13 major titles between 1923–30. His second name is, however, convincing evidence that there was Welsh in there somewhere. Who was he?

81. This woman goes round the world, largely on her own and faster than most men who travel in the same way. Despite many websites which give information on her, it is difficult to find out where she was born, but rumour has it one or both of her parents are Welsh. Is this enough to qualify and, if so, who is she?

History

One country can't really have *more* history than another country. All places have been around for the same length of time, whatever they got called along the way, and something was going on everywhere even if we don't know what it was. However, Wales seems to manage the impossible of having more history than it should have, and what is more, it seems to have better history! It has more drama, more variety, it has good history, unhappy endings, villains, twists and plots; it is, well – better, more interesting. Of course a lot depends on just what you call history; if you mean dry, provable facts with plenty of evidence to back them up well – OK. But if you mean what happened, or could have happened, or *should* have happened… Well, it depends on what you mean by history, doesn't it?

1. Everyone in Wales was asked to go to the polls in 1997. What were they voting about?

2. What group of Welshmen responded to the call of 'King Arthur' but did it in 1984?

3. Brunel finally got Cardiff connected to Bristol via the Great Western Railway in 1841. What engineering feat did he complete in that year to make it possible?

4. What did an Empress spill off Pembroke in 1996?

5. A man aged about 21 and known as the Red Lady of Paviland lived in the Gower Peninsula. What is his claim to fame?

6. It must be the only one of its kind in the world brought into being by a hunger strike. What did Gwynfor Evans, leader of Plaid Cymru, threaten to starve for, and get for Wales in 1982?

7. Aneurin, Taliesin and Llywarch Hen were all busy in Wales during 5–600AD. What were they?

8. Farmers in drag were all the rage between 1839–44. They specialised in knocking down gates. What sort of gates did they smash?

9. Who paid his first visit to Wales in 1081?

10. Over 60,000 new kinds of Welshmen appeared overnight in Wales in 1867. What were they?

11. When did Wales get its own Welsh Language Radio programmes?
    a) 1912
    b) 1934
    c) 1952
    d) 1968
    e) 1977

12. When did Wales get its own English Language Radio programmes?
    a) 1912
    b) 1934
    c) 1952
    d) 1968
    e) 1977

13. Llewelyn Fawr – Llewelyn the Great – was well-named, a great leader and a true Prince of Wales. When did he die?
    a) 1170
    b) 1240
    c) 1312
    d) 1381
    e) 1407

14. How long did it take the UK Parliament to allow Welsh MPs to take their oath in Welsh as well as English.
    a) 400 years
    b) 300 years
    c) 200 years
    d) 100 years
    e) they still can't

15. Where in Wales was described in 1847 as a... 'solitudinous and happy valley... where a Sabbath stillness reigns', yet by the 1850s was described as 'a vision of hell'!

16. The biggest fire since the Fire of London, lasting 18 days, happened at Pembroke Dock. Fire engines from as far away as Cardiff were called out. Who started it?

17. A Welsh speaking valley was drowned in 1957, sanctioned by Act of Parliament. Why?

18. In 1881 Wales' greatest and perhaps most powerful union was founded. Which one?

19. In 1974 Wales lost 13 but got 8 – of what?

20. Seren Gomer (The Star of Gomer) came from Swansea, only survived through Wales for one year but came again in different forms in 1818 and 1820. What was it?

21. 1966 may have been a golden year for English football but a tragedy happened in a South Wales valley which made it one of Wales' darkest years. What was it?

22. Thomas Telford celebrated the defeat of Napoleon at Waterloo in Betws y Coed in the same year as the battle,1815. How did he celebrate the victory?

23. Wales got its first taste of Bubonic plague around what time (All dates are AD)?
    a) 50
    b) 550
    c) 800
    d) 1090
    e) 1413

24. In 1813 Welsh insurrectionists fought Highland troops in what became known as the Merthyr Rising. There was loss of life on both sides. What was raised for the first time in Britain during this rebellion?

25. The members of which Society sat down and blocked traffic in Aberystwyth in support of their demands in 1963?

26. A group of French irregulars under an American General went off course and landed and surrendered at Fishguard in 1797. What made this odd little incident so special?

27. Dr. Hugh Price chose Jesus as the name for his foundation in 1571. What was it he founded?

28. When did Wales get its own Secretary of State?
    a) 1903
    b) 1919
    c) 1935
    d) 1954
    e) 1964

29. When was the first book printed in Welsh?
    a) 1493
    b) 1547
    c) 1601
    d) 1650
    e) 1725.

30. Has there ever been a Welsh Home Rule Bill presented to the Commons by an MP?

31. What did Bishop Morgan give to the Welsh people in their own language?

32. What did the Welsh do in England in 1917 and again in 1929?

33. When was Cardiff officially declared the capital of Wales?
    a) 1287
    b) 1469
    c) 1536
    d) 1825
    e) 1955

34. What killed around 10,000 people in Wales between 1918–19?

35. The Church of Wales, unlike The Church of England, is disestablished. What year did this happen?
    a) 1899
    b) 1914
    c) 1920
    d) 1925
    e) 1931

36. In 1887 the Blackstone Eisteddfod was held and established a tradition of Eisteddfods. Where did it take place?

37. What was first raised in England in 1689 and went on to become Wales' oldest today?

38.   When was the first Welsh language broadcast made by the BBC?
- a) 1927
- b) 1935
- c) 1941
- d) 1945
- e) 1956

39.   Why is the area around the Welsh–English borders called 'The Marches'?

40.   What year was Plaid Cymru, the National Party of Wales, formed?
- a) 1899
- b) 1916
- c) 1925
- d) 1931
- e) 1945

41.   Who sent armed British troops to restore order during the Tonypandy Riots of 1910 in South Wales?

42.   The Welsh parish of Gresford has a grave with the bodies of over 250 men in it. Why?

43.   What year did Lloyd George become Prime Minister?
- a) 1910
- b) 1912
- c) 1914
- d) 1916
- e) 1917

44. In 1893 it became possible to stay at home in Wales and get what instead of going to London?

45. When did Cardiff get city status?
    a) 1899
    b) 1905
    c) 1914
    d) 1920
    e) 1955

46. Where was The Miners' Federation of Great Britain founded in 1889?
    a) Cardiff
    b) Merthyr Tydfil
    c) Neath
    d) Newport
    e) Swansea

47. Who made it 155 world-wide when they came to Cardiff in 2003 with the UK's second largest?

48. What radical change to Welsh tradition did Gwynedd Council try to bring about on a quiet stretch of beach in 2001?

49. Who paid their first visit to Wales in 48AD?

50. It began in 1900 at Penrhyn and finished in 1903 and was for many years the longest what in British history?

51. Which Welsh-speaking Mancunian first turned up for work at Westminster in 1890?

52. Who celebrated Mabon's Monday on the first Monday of each month in the late 1800s?

53. What turned up in Haverfordwest in 1652 for the last time but killed 400 people?

54. Who did Seutonius Paulinas have a go at in AD 59 on Anglesey?

55. When did the *Western Mail* newspaper first come off the presses?
    a) 1783
    b) 1815
    c) 1869
    d) 1898
    e) 1905

56. What did Gerald of Wales, Archdeacon of Brecon, do around the 12th century which made him famous?

57. In 1752 Richard Morris wrote to the Bishop of Bangor that '...the mad _____ have bewitched the major part of the inhabitants.' Who was he writing about?

58. Who united in 1873 in South Wales to give themselves more industrial muscle?

59.   In 1782 a customs official said, 'We have no coal exported from this port nor ever shall.' Which port was he referring to?
   a)   Cardiff
   b)   Fishguard
   c)   Holyhead
   d)   Milford Haven
   e)   Swansea.

60.   Merthyr Tydfil and Swansea lost over 300 people when they were the unlucky hosts to the first UK visit of what in 1832?

61.   Llanelli and Pontarddulais shared in a piece of Welsh history in 1839. What was the link?

62.   An important annual date stopped being Welsh and became Roman in 768 AD. What was it the date of?

63.   In 1984 the Welsh word for 'to keep' – 'cadw' – became the name of an official Welsh Agency. What does it do?

64.   Where was chosen as the most appropriate site for the Wales Waterfront Museum, which celebrates the history of Welsh sea trading?

65.   Wales got its first official town when? (dates are all AD)
   a)   120
   b)   943
   c)   1172
   d)   1312
   e)   1536

66. How many Welsh-speakers lived in Wales at the beginning of the 21st century (to the nearest 5,000)?
    a) 25,000
    b) 40,000
    c) 65,000
    d) 130,000
    e) 550,000

67. The English have a long history of taking away Welsh natural resources for their own use. One of the earliest examples happened around 3000BC when they came to Wales looking for suitable building materials. What were they building?

68. When were the Welsh Guards first raised?
    a) 1645
    b) 1743
    c) 1813
    d) 1879
    e) 1915

69. It is a tradition of British Royal Family marriages that a little bit of Wales is always used in the ceremony. What part does it play?

70. Born illegitimate in Denbigh in 1841 he was brought up in the workhouse before going off to New Orleans to seek his fortune. In New Orleans he changed his name and in 1871 achieved fame for finding someone who wasn't lost. Who was he?

71. The Museum of Welsh Life at St. Fagans was first opened when?
   a) 1939
   b) 1948
   c) 1956
   d) 1975
   e) 2000

72. The famous son of a Covent Garden wig maker and barber toured south Wales in the 1790s to brush up on his drawing skills. Who was he?
   a) William Blake
   b) John Constable
   c) George Morland
   d) William Pitt
   e) William Turner

73. Between 1070 and 1300 the Normans established around 80 what across Wales?
   a) abbeys
   b) castles
   c) convents
   d) religious shrines
   e) towns

74. 10th century Wales had some of the most enlightened laws in Europe for a certain class of people allowing them to exercise limited rights of property and recognising they had some family rights. What members of society were they?

75. Rhodri Mawr (the Great) scored a Welsh first around 942 AD. What was his achievement?

76. Henry VIII tried to kill off something Welsh (not a wife) when he created the 'Act of Union'. What did he want dead?

77. Who was the great Welshman who nearly gave Wales back to the Welsh between 1354–1416?

78. The preferred system of transport in late 18th century Wales was horse-drawn. Somebody estimated that one horse, under the right conditions, could pull a load of around 25 tons. What were these right conditions?

79. What did Wales vote on and reject in 1979?

80. It was all over in 1944 because, among a cast of 60, the fat lady sang and Wales' own what finally came into being?

Trivia

Wales isn't a trivial country but it does throw up a lot of odd bits and pieces of information. Trivia are small and unimportant things, items or bits of information. Of course one person's trivia may well be another person's treasure, so what properly constitutes trivia is difficult to judge. There's all sorts in this section – films and film stars, music and musicians, writers and writing, art and artists, and it may seem that some of the questions concern things that are anything but trivial. However, there is, I think, one really good reason why anything can go in this section and that is because this is just a Quiz Book and, as such, is about as trivial as you can get!

1. The letter value (without using any premium squares) of which name has a higher score in Scrabble, Cardiff or Swansea?

2. What is it that Welsh men, after 65, do more often than Welsh women?

3. What is the second most common Welsh surname supposed to be?

4. How did Clint Eastwood give Wales a bad name in Hollywood in 1976?

5. What would you call a Welsh Goon?

6. The tycoon Arthur Mc Dougall built a holiday home at Fairbourne getting it started as a resort. What did he make his money in?

7. How did someone lose £1.9 million in Wales in 2002?

8. What, according to the 2001 Census, is the most common form of accommodation in Wales? Detached house, flat, semi-detached house, terraced house, other.

9. What was Wales most popular adult crime during the Millennium year?

10. In 2001 Welsh families found they topped the UK averages with what domestic problem?

11. What American catastrophe gave rise to the Tal-y-llyn narrow-gauge Railway at Tywyn in 1865?

12. Two brothers, grandsons of a Baptist Minister from Pembroke, made it really big in America. Who were they?

13. Actress Nia Roberts read the poem 'His Requiem' in a reading of poems by Dylan Thomas as part of the BBC celebrations of the 50th anniversary of his death. The *Western Mail* objected. Why?

14. The English 'Iron Ring' of Wales has been given World Heritage status. What is it?

15. In 2003 at the Anuga International Food Festival the firm Murroughs of Swansea scooped deals with outlets in Australia, Germany, Canada and Belgium to supply – what?

16. Which Welshman's eating habits came as a nasty shock to everyone in 1990?

17. 'Cwm Rhondda' or 'Guide Me Oh Thou Great Redeemer' is sung on such state occasions such as Rugby Internationals. Who wrote it?

18. A Welsh lad 'Walked on Air' to a big hit. Who was he?

19. A new religion appeared in the 2001 census, claiming an average 0.7% of the population of England and Wales. It was most popular in Brighton and Hove with 2.6% but least popular in Merthyr Tydfil with only 0.2 adherents. What was the new religion?

20. If you were allowed one double letter score, which would score more at Scrabble – Wales or Cymru?

21. Which Welsh actor said he had to stay sober to play drunks because he couldn't play them when he was drunk himself?

22. Who started aged 10 in a talent contest in Butlins but became 'Catherine the Great' on TV in 1995?

23. Where did they feel least healthy in Wales in 2001? Blaenau (Gwent), Caerphilly, Merthyr Tydfil, Neath or the Rhondda.

24. Ivor Emmanuel helped fight off the Zulus at Rorke's Drift with Stanley Baker and Michael Caine. What else did he do for a living?

25. This Welsh comedian and actor was, Alas, half of a pair who flopped as 'Morons from Outer Space'. Who was he?

26. Sir Henry Morgan was a famous Welsh what?

27. When was the last steam-hauled public service railway line opened in Wales?
    a) 1927
    b) 1936
    c) 1941
    d) 1952
    e) 1997

28. The famous Welsh duo Augustus and Gwen John made their names as what?

29. Which famous Welshman had to wait around 500 years for his first biography to come out to the public?

30. Tredegar Working Men's Medical Aid Association was the model for which post-war wonder of the world?

31. What does Bryn Terfel do to earn his pay packet?

32. The readers of *Melody Maker* voted three Welsh boys Sexiest Rockers of 1998. Which two groups did they belong to?

33. It took Bernard Thomas 13½ hours to cross the English Channel in 1974. How did he cross?

34. What did the Ladies of Llangollen create between 1780 and 1831 which is still a joy today?

35. At Clynnog Fawr, on the Llŷn Peninsula, is St. Beuno's Well. A local custom, that lasted up until the 1800s, said that any animal born bearing Beuno's mark had to – what?

36. If you were to come across some Ogam in Wales what would you be looking at?

37. It is claimed that the film stars Keanu Reeves and Gene Hackman both have a favourite Welsh drink. What is it?

38. How do we know that the cod, the hake and the grey mullet all thrive in Welsh coastal waters?

39. What was opened in Wales to celebrate the Millennium in 2000, the first of its kind for over 200 years?

40. What percentage of people living in Wales in 2001 thought they were Welsh (to the nearest 10%)?

41. Who was Marcellus Gallio in 1953, Mark Anthony in 1963 and finished up in Room 101 in 1984?

42. For what Welsh product could 'Brains are what it takes' be the motto?

43. Who did Little Tommy Woodward from Treforest turn into when he borrowed a name from Henry Fielding?

44. War correspondent Wynford Vaughan Thomas scored a first in 1944 which could easily have killed him. What was it?

45. James Bond married the daughter of a steel worker from south Wales. Who was she?

46. The last working one in Wales is on Anglesey. What is it?

47. 'So far as I'm concerned they are lower than vermin'. Strong words from Aneurin 'Nye' Bevan – who was he talking about?

48. Two famous American outlaws, on the run at the beginning of the 20th century, found safety among the Welsh. Who were the outlaws?

49. Which Welsh Eliza did it three times for James Bond?

50. Which Scotsman, played by an Australian in an American film was known as the 'Welshman'?

51. A Welsh choir was taken to court by Rees Lloyd and Geraint Wilkes for 'false advertising' and forced to state that it was, in fact, a multi-ethnic choir in its promotional literature. There's only one place on earth where this sort of thing goes on. Where is it?

52. Gruffudd Gwenwynwyn regained Powis Castle when he returned from exile in England with Edward I and his army. His son, Owain, kept the castle in the family on Gruffudd's death but the family lost what in the process?

53. 'Er cof am' is one of the most used written phrases in Welsh, occurring all over Wales. Where would you expect to find it?

54. How many of the old 13 Welsh counties can you name? Better than 9 is OK (especially if you're under 30).

55. 'The Biological Utilisation of Quantum Non-Locality' never became a best seller nor did it get serialised in the *News of the World* for Welsh physicist Brian Josephson. But he did manage to pick up what for his work?

56. Famous as a writer for children, a short story writer and a screenwriter, he gave TV 'Tales of the Unexpected' in 1979. He was born in Llandaf in 1916 and died of leukaemia in 1990. Who was he?

57. Billy Meredith from Black Park, North Wales, is claimed as the first super-star of which sport?
    a) cycling
    b) football
    c) motor-cycling
    d) rugby
    e) snooker

58. It is in Conway, and is only 72 inches wide and 122 inches high and is probably the smallest of its kind in the UK. What is it?

59. They call themselves 'The finest Welsh Male Voice Choir in Asia' on their web-site. They were founded in 1978. Where do they sing?

60. The Old House pub in Llangynwyd, Maesteg, won the Good Pub Guide's UK award for what drink in 2001?

61. Cardiff Council helps run an annual competition with a first prize of £5000. What would you have to do to win?

62. A Llanelli lad grew up to become the politician who did away with the trade union closed shop, and as Home Secretary, he was famous for telling everyone that 'prison works'. Having gone into the political wilderness, he bounced back in 2003 to be Tory Party leader. Who was he?

63. It's said to be the biggest of its kind in the world and you can have a look through it in Aberystwyth. What is it?

64. He was born David Ivor Davies in 1893 in Cardiff. His father, David Davies, was a tax collector, but he took his mother's maiden name and became famous as 'the Last Great Romantic', and gave his name to a well-known awards ceremony. Who was he?

65. The earliest known example of one of these dates back to 1677 and is kept at the Museum of Welsh Life in Cardiff. It is a peculiarly Welsh way of declaring your love. What is it?

66. On what special occasion is kidnapping considered legal in Wales?

67. The hip commentators of the 1990s felt Wales was really swinging and producing so much great young talent that they came up with a name for Wales which they felt really said it all. They took their cue from Tony Blair and declared that, to them, Wales was – what?

68. What do you always get two-for-the-price-of-one in Wales, but not in England?

69. Which does Wales have more of, natural lakes or reservoirs?

70. According to the RSPB's Big Garden Birdwatch, which was Wales' most common garden bird of 2003?

71. What did Wales celebrate on 12th January each year up until 1752?

72. Jon Gower of BBC Wales said that Wales had come a long way since a secret Catholic printing press was thought to have been used in a cave in Llandudno some 500 years ago. What aspect of Welsh communication was he talking about?

73. Owain Glyndŵr sparked yet another revolt in Wales, but this time it was in Aberystwyth in 2003 and pitched the Chamber of Commerce against Ceredigion Council. The battle was over part of North Parade. What did the Council want to do?

74. According to the listings of English-wine.com how many commercial vineyards did Wales have in 2003?

75. Welsh family brewers Felinfoel scored a European first in 1935 when they produced – what?

76. How does the Welsh version of Scrabble differ from the English one?

77. Which 20th century Welsh philosopher wrote 'A History of Western Philosophy'?

78. In 1942 Colwyn Bay gave a Python to the world. Which one?

79. Gilbern was once the name of a Welsh product – alas, now defunct. What was it?
    a) beer
    b) breakfast cereal
    c) car
    d) gin
    e) waterproof coat

80. Which meat is used in a traditional Glamorgan sausage?

Answers

Places Answers

1. c) Capel Curig in Snowdonia.

2. e) Llanwrtyd Wells – beer and bog snorkelling.

3. Flintshire in the north east corner of Wales.

4. The three national capitals closest to St. David's measured as the crow flies are (to the nearest 5 units of measure): Cardiff 90 km – 55 miles, Dublin 100km – 60 miles and London 220km – 140 miles.

5. d) 1923. Although St. John's Church was founded in the 11th century as a priory it didn't become a Diocese until the Disestablishment of the Church of Wales and the creation of the new Brecon and Swansea Diocese in 1923.

6. d) Highest proportion of under 16-year-olds is Newport (Gwent) with 22.5%.

7. c) Swansea and i) Shrewsbury.

8. Big Pit, at Blaenavon, once a working colliery.

9. d) Llanthony, the anglicised version of Llantoni, which is in turn the shortened version of the full Welsh name, Llanddewi Nant Hodni. The name is nothing to do with anyone called Anthony, saint or otherwise.

10. c) 1800. The grave was erected by an enterprising hotel owner who wanted to promote the tourist trade.

11.   c) The Holy Grail, the cup said to be used by Jesus at the Last Supper. No-one knows how it may have reached Wales, although there are stories that it made its way there from Glastonbury.

12.   e) Rhyl.

13.   b) Merthyr Tydfil. They elected the Scot, Kier Hardie, in 1900, the same year the Labour Party came into being.

14.   d) The Church of Peter by the bridge of Stephen!

15.   They distilled Welsh whiskey. Whiskey was once produced throughout Wales, but the industry got knocked on the head by the Temperance Movement within the Non-Conformist Churches.

16.   Plynlimon in the Cambrian Mountains, inland between Aberystwyth and Aberdovey.

17.   a) Bardsey Island, off the tip of the Lleyn Peninsula in north west Wales.

18.   The River Teifi.

19.   Llyn Tegid.

20.   c) Holywell, which is home to St. Winifride's Well near the north Wales coast.

21.   a) Chepstow is the oldest, begun in 1067, but strangely it has seen comparatively little action in its long life.

22.   The Menai Suspension Bridge built in 1826.

23.   Thomas Telford.

24.   e) Chepstow at the southern end, and h) Prestatyn at the northern end.

25.   a) Pryce Pryce-Jones was, in fact, the father of mail order shopping which he began on a commercial scale to supply the local widely scattered rural community.

26.   b) Mount Everest. It was given its modern English name in 1865 in honour of Sir George Everest, Surveyor General in India, following its identification as the highest point on the globe by a British Indian government survey in 1852. Sir George was born in Breconshire.

27.   c) Caldey Island off the Pembroke coast. The original monastery was Celtic but the Benedictines arrived from St. Dogmael's in the 12th century.

28.   e) It happened in Machynlleth in west mid-Wales.

29.   e) His grave is in the churchyard of St. Giles, the parish church of Wrexham.

30.   b) Llandrindod Wells was the biggest, and it now hosts a popular annual Victorian Week when everyone dresses up in period costume and goes back in time to celebrate the great days of the 19th century.

31.   b) The Llŷn Peninsula in north west Wales. Lawrence was born at Tremadog.

32.   d) 1926.

33.   e) A bog. Tregaron Bog, just north of Lampeter, is the best example of a raised bog in Europe. The river Teifi provides the water and it is home to a nature reserve of almost 2000 acres.

34.   Hay-on-Wye where they've even turned the old cinema into a second-hand bookshop.

35.   a) Carmarthen.

36. Pendine Sands, a long flat stretch of beach in the middle of the Carmarthen Bay coast.

37. a) He and his wife Caitlin ate and slept in the Boat House.

38. Charles was invested as Prince of Wales in 1969 at Caernarfon castle.

39. Wales' highest waterfall is Pistyll Rhaeadr. It is just in Clwyd, on the southern edge of the Berwyn Mountains in mid-Wales.

40. a) Aberystwyth has always been the home of the National Library of Wales since its beginning in 1907.

41. d) The investiture took place at Lincoln in 1301.

42. a) Beaumaris, begun in 1295. Edward 1st died in 1307.

43. b) 1826 by Thomas Telford.

44. d) 168 miles.

45. a) It means 'big kitchen'. It was once the place where the local church provided meals and hospitality to pilgrims on their way to Bardsey Island.

46. b) Slate quarry. At its height it was the biggest open-cast slate quarry in the world and employed over 3000 men.

47. e) Most is Powys with 0.98 men per woman, next is Flintshire with 0.96 then Monmouth and Bridgend with 0.95 and finally Anglesey where each woman only gets 0.94 of a man!

48. d) Llangollen which is closer to the border than its neighbour, Corwen.

49. Cardiff 305,000, Swansea 223,000 Newport 137.000 Wrexham 128,000 Holyhead 12,000 (to the nearest 1000 from Census 2001)

50. c) Merthyr Tydfil with a population of 8000. At that time Cardiff's population was only around 2000.

51. The total coastline of Wales extends to around 600 miles.

52. d) Chapel in the wood.

53. The wettest place (in a normal year) is on the very top of Mount Snowdon with an annual rainfall of 340cm per year.

54. Almost, but not quite. You have to nip into England via Shrewsbury before going back into Wales and on to Swansea.

55. c) 170 miles.

56. It varies, of course, but it is around 80%. Any answer between 75%–85% should be regarded as correct.

57. a) It's in Argentina, part of a Welsh settlement in Patagonia.

58. 20,000 sq. km.

59. c) St. Asaph's in mid north Wales, a few miles inland from Rhyl. It sits between two rivers, the Conwy and the Elwy.

60. 3560 ft. so any answer between 3460ft and 3660ft. is OK.

61. Rorke's Drift in 1879 in South Africa.

62. b) An aircraft runway and maintenance facility.

63. Milford Haven in Pembrokeshire, which is still a busy major oil terminal.

64. The River Usk.

65. Caerleon, not far from Newport (Gwent), which has a very good museum of the Roman history of the town.

66. The River Taff.

67. Caerphilly.

68. The Dee estuary.

69. c) Carnedd Llewelyn at 3484ft. The others are: Carnedd Dafydd 3426ft., Glyder Fawr 3278ft. Tryfan 3010ft. and Cader Idris 2927ft.

70. Porthmadog.

71. b) Cardiff Castle. It was presented to the people of Cardiff in 1947 and is now looked after by the Council.

72. The largest of the old Welsh counties was, and still is, Carmarthenshire.

73. The river Clwyd.

74. The Dovey Valley.

75. The Elan Valley Waterworks, a system of dams and man-made lakes covering an area of roughly 71 sq. miles.

76. South Pembroke, so called because of the English settlement that was established in Norman times.

77. Welshpool.

78. The River Tawe.

79. The Brecon Beacons National Park, the Pembroke Coast National Park and the Snowdonia National Park.

80. e) Radnorshire situated about half way down Wales on the border with England.

81. They stand at each end of the Gower Peninsula.

82. e) 2002.

Sport Answers

1. Badminton. Kelly, a former Commonwealth Champion, beat Korea's Eun Woo Lee 13–10, 7–11, 11–5 to pick up the title.

2. Cycling. They got the new national Velodrome.

3. A fantastic 15 titles.

4. Rugby, or more accurately Women's Rugby. Llandaf North scooped the Women's Rugby national Cup, the National League title and the South Division 1 title.

5. Rowing. Ivor held the Cross Channel Rowing record for 20 years until Guin Batten, a fellow Leander Rowing Club member, took it off him in 2003.

6. 1981.

7. Eric was a darts player.

8. Archery. Compound refers to the bow used.

9. It took 59 years for Welsh women to get their own Athletics Championships after the men's Championships were established. The men got theirs in 1893 whereas the women had to wait until 1952.

10. Motor racing. Pembrey, a derelict airfield had been turned into a commercial chicken farm, but was abandoned when it was bought by Llanelli Borough Council who agreed to develop the site into a racing circuit with the newly formed Welsh Racing Drivers Association.

11. Colin broke the record at a Wrexham meeting.

12. Cricket. Wales is a Minor County side whilst Glamorgan is a County Cricket side.

13. Sandra went to the ochie for Wales at Darts.

14. Motor racing.

15. 1977. The other two members of the Welsh team were Alan Evans and David Jones.

16. Cycling. Nicole scooped the title with a 5th place finish in Nuremberg. That was ahead of all of her rivals for the title and good enough to win the overall Cup Series.

17. Formula 1 motor racing.

18. Wales got its own Cricket Association in 1969.

19. Angela was a distance runner and her National records were in the; 3000 metres set in Stockholm, 5000 metres set in Oslo and 10,000 metres set in Rome.

20. Cycling.

21. Gary hit six sixes for Nottingham when they played against Glamorgan in Swansea.

22. The year Ian Woosnam picked up the Green Jacket at the Masters was 1991.

23. This unusual qualifying match was played against Israel.

24. Cliff was playing Terry Griffiths, though most people who saw the match on TV remember fellow-Canadian Bill Werbeniuk's face peeping round the dividing screen rather than Terry sitting in his chair as Cliff edged towards the total.

25. The Welsh jump jockey Carl Llewellyn was the man who subbed to two wins in the Grand National.

26. It was a winner in the TV series Robot Wars.

27. 1993.

28. It was Leeds who picked up the Juventus cash for John Charles.

29. Gareth was captain of Wales 13 times.

30. John was born in Swansea in 1975.

31. National Village Championships cricket final.

32. They were deaf. The tournament was the Deaf Rugby Championships.

33. Wrexham.

34. Women's Ice Hockey.

35. Glamorgan.

36. Horse Racing.

37. Legs.

38. Terry picked up the title in 1979.

39. Cardiff beat Arsenal to win the FA cup.

40. Lyn made his jump for gold in 1964.

41. Ray was a miner.

42. The County Cricket Championship. Glamorgan beat Somerset in the final.

43. Sirrell entered Norton's Coin at the last minute for the Cheltenham Gold Cup and the horse was a surprise winner.

44. Tommy was fighting the immortal Joe Louis for the heavyweight world crown. Joe beat him but to go the distance with probably the greatest heavyweight ever was still a magnificent achievement.

45. The Football Association of Wales is the third oldest in the world and was founded in 1876.

46. The Grand National.

47. John Toshack.

48. Joe Calzaghe beat Chris Ewbank before going on to his boxing world title.

49. Sheep-shearing.

50. Women's cricket.

51. The Welsh lacrosse team.

52. Wales got its first club golf course.

53. Howard was a boxer.

54. Wales got its governing body for swimming in 1897.

55. The Welsh Hockey Union.

56. The 'they' were Terry Griffiths and Cliff Thorburn again and they were playing snooker in the Embassy World Championships.

57. This sorry tale is the story of Newport County's 87–88 season.

58. This piece of rugby history belongs to Newport, who tackled everything that moved on the day and scored the only points of the match with a drop goal that hit the bar before toppling over to give Newport the win.

59.   Hugh was the TV commentator for ITV. Everyone remembers Ken Wolstenholme's BBC commentary, 'They think it's all over… *England score…* it is now…' but no-one seems to have been watching the match on ITV or, if they did, no-one remembers what Hugh said at the critical moment.

60.   Wales had four amateur winners in the 80's; Duncan Evans 1980, Phillip Parkin 1983, Paul Mayo 1987 and Stephen Dodd 1989.

61.   Chess.

62.   Swansea. Georgio was Italian but grew up in Swansea.

63.   Formula 1 power boat racing.

64.   Matthew Stevens.

65.   The Walker Cup, the amateur golf competition played between the US and the UK and Ireland.

66.   Show jumping.

67.   Bowls.

68.   Retractable roof.

69.   Canoes.

70.   The Stableford scoring system.

71.   Dick Francis.

72.   It was the needle valve used to inflate sports balls.

73.   Tanni's sport was paralympics as a wheelchair race athlete.

74.   Snooker.

75.   Rugby.

76.   Chepstow.

The 'almost Welsh' list:

77.   Vinnie Jones.

78.   David Gower.

79.   Jacques Kallis.

80.   Bobby Jones.

81.   Tracy Edwards.

History Answers

1. Devolution.

2. The Miners. The 'King' in question was miners' leader Arthur Scargill.

3. The rail tunnel under the Severn.

4. The oil tanker the Sea Empress grounded off Pembroke creating a massive oil-spill.

5. He's about 24,000 years old.

6. A Welsh Language TV channel – SC4.

7. Poets or bards.

8. Toll gates. They took part in the Rebecca Riots. In these riots the men dressed up in women's clothes to protest against excessive rural tolls. The name they chose, Rebecca and her Daughters, may have reflected their strenuous Christianity and have been taken from a biblical quote, "*possess the gates of those which hate them*". (Genesis XXIV, 60).

9. William the Conqueror.

10. Voters. In 1867 all male householders were given the right to vote in the UK creating a massive new electorate. Women, of course, weren't included and had to wait for their opinions to matter.

11. 1977.

12. 1977.

13. 1240.

14. 400 years. The right wasn't granted until 1974.

15. Rhondda Valley. It was turned from a quiet rural backwater with just a few inhabitants into a crowded industrial nightmare in just a few short years.

16. The Luftwaffe.

17. A Welsh village was evacuated and submerged by a reservoir to provide safe drinking water for Liverpool.

18. The Welsh Rugby Union.

19. Counties. They lost the 13 old shire counties and got 8 new super-counties.

20. The first Welsh language weekly newspaper.

21. The terrible Aberfan tragedy. On 21 October part of a mountain of coal waste slipped into the village and covered a village primary school, with the loss of life of 144 people, 116 of them children. The resulting enquiry into the disaster concluded that… 'the Aberfan Disaster is a terrifying tale of bungling ineptitude by many men charged with tasks for which they were totally unfitted…'

22. By naming the A5 road-bridge he built there the Waterloo Bridge.

23. 550.

24. The Red Flag.

25. The Welsh Language Society.

26. It was the last invasion of the British mainland.

27. Jesus College, Oxford.

28. 1964.

29. 1547.

30. Yes. A home rule for Wales Bill was put before Parliament by E. T. John, member for Denbigh. No-one noticed and it got nowhere, but at least he tried.

31. The Bible.

32. They held the National Eisteddfod at Birkenhead in 1917 and at Liverpool in 1929.

33. The Act of Union declared Wales to be part of England and, therefore, not entitled to a national capital. That stayed the way of things until 1955 when Cardiff became the official capital of Wales.

34. Influenza.

35. 1920. Parliament actually passed the Bill in 1914 but implementation was delayed by the war.

36. Australia in the Ipswich coalfields. It began the tradition of Australian Eisteddfods.

37. The Royal Welch Fusilliers. They were raised in Ludlow and saw their first action in Ireland at the Battle of the Boyne.

38. 1935.

39. The name "March" is derived from the Anglo-Saxon "mearc," which means "boundary."

40. 1925.

41. Winston Churchill.

42. Because in 1934 Gresford suffered a terrible pit disaster. It proved impossible to retrieve the bodies of over 250 of the miners so the pit was sealed and became their tomb.

43. 1916.

44. A University Degree. A University of Wales Charter was granted to three Welsh colleges which could then confer degrees.

45. Cardiff became a city in 1955.

46. Newport.

47. IKEA.

48. They tried to set up Wales' first official nudist beach. It was opened for a trial year against considerable local opposition.

49. The Romans.

50. Strike or industrial dispute.

51. David Lloyd George as MP for Caernarfon. There was an unexpected by-election in 1890 with the death of the sitting Tory member, Edmund Swetenham. Lloyd George won the seat with a majority of 18 and only after a recount. However, after that he never looked back and won a series of fourteen elections which he fought between 1890 and 1945.

52. South Wales miners. William Abraham (Mabon) was a miners' leader who managed to keep the industrial peace for around 20 years and actually got some better conditions for them. He entered Parliament in 1885.

53. Bubonic plague.

54. The Druids. He thought they were behind continued Welsh resistance to Roman occupation so attacked their stronghold in Anglesey and destroyed what was left of their power.

55. 1869.

56. He wrote about Wales and is now known by his Latin name Giraldus Cambrensis. His two books, 'A Journey through Wales' and 'A Description of Wales' remain two of the very few written sources from the period.

57. Methodists, who were converting the working-class Welsh in droves.

58. The South Wales Coal Owners who became the Monmouth and South Wales Coal-owners Association.

59. Cardiff. This far-sited official felt that it would never be economical to transport valley coal all the way to Cardiff. He was wrong. By 1907 Cardiff was the biggest coal exporting port in the world.

60. Cholera.

61. They were at either end of the first railway built in Wales designed to take locomotives.

62. Easter. The Welsh, like the Northern English and the Scots and Irish, kept the Celtic date for Easter. When Augustine came from Rome to Southern England to convert the Saxons he brought the Roman date with him. It was changed for the English Church at the Synod of Whitby in 664 but the Welsh held out for the old date before finally having to come into line with Rome.

63. It looks after Welsh Monuments and Historic buildings.

64. Swansea.

65. Wales achieved its first official town in 120 AD when the Roman settlement of Caerwent was granted the status of 'civitas' or a provincial capital.

66. 550,000 out of a population of approximately 3 million.

67. Stonehenge. Some of the Blue Stone used for Stonehenge came from the Preseli Mountains in Wales.

68. 1915.

69.   Welsh gold is traditionally used for the wedding rings.

70.   Henry Morton Stanley. He found the explorer and missionary Livingstone who was very ill but not lost. He was born the illegitimate son of John Rowlands but took the name Stanley from a merchant in New Orleans who befriended him.

71.   1948.

72.   William Turner.

73.   Towns.

74.   Women. Married women, under Welsh law, retained certain rights over their own property and were allowed some say in the bringing up of their children. Married women in England had to wait until the 19th century to get rights over their own property.

75.   He unified Wales under one ruler.

76.   The Welsh language. He made it an important part of the 'Act of Union' that no Welsh speaker could hold any public office. As almost everyone in Wales was, at that time, a Welsh speaker you don't have to be a genius to see what he was getting at.

77.   Owain Glyndŵr.

78.   Canals. One horse could pull about 5 tons on a good rood surface but one horse could pull five times that weight along a canal. This simple fact led to much canal building in South Wales.

79.   Devolution. There was a referendum and Wales said 'No'.

80.   The Welsh National Opera held its first rehearsal.

1. Cardiff wins with 16 points, C scoring 3, A R and I scoring 1 each and F scoring 4. Swansea gets 10 points, 1 for S A N and E with 4 for W.

2. Die. The death rate of Welsh men compared to women rises rapidly after 65, going up to three times as great when they pass 80.

3. It is supposed to be Davies.

4. He used the name Wales for an outlaw character in the film, 'The Outlaw Josey Wales'.

5. Harry Secombe.

6. Flour.

7. They didn't claim the winning lottery ticket.

8. The semi-detached house, with terraced housing running it a close second and detached houses not far behind in third. Flats were a strong fourth, but 'other' was a distant last.

9. If 'Those given an Official Police Caution as a percentage of those found guilty or given a caution' can be used as a reliable index then the most popular adult (over 18) crime of the Millennium Year was; Theft and handling Stolen Goods.

10. Debt.

11. The American Civil War. The outbreak of the Civil War dried up the supply of raw cotton so Manchester cotton

manufacturers sought new investments to create income. The Talyllyn Railway was a project to bring slate down to the coast for export.

12. Frank and Jesse James, whose gang is credited with the very first US daylight bank robbery.

13. He didn't write it. He saw it in the *Boy's Own* as a lad, and submitted it to the *Western Mail* as his own work. They gave him ten bob and published it. The *Mail* discovered their mistake when somebody wrote in and told them it was first published in the *Boy's Own*. However, by the time this was discovered, it had got into Thomas' collected works and still, as the BBC found out, gets wrongly attributed to him.

14. The system of medieval castles designed to subdue the Welsh.

15. Welsh Tea.

16. Anthony Hopkins for his portrayal of Hannibal Lecter in 'Silence of the Lambs'.

17. John Hughes (1873–1932)

18. Aled Jones.

19. Jedi – which first appeared in the film Star Wars.

20. The best score you could get with Wales would be 12 by doubling the W. Cymru, however, would get you 16 if you doubled the Y.

21. Richard Burton.

22. Catherine Zeta Jones.

23. The 2001 Census revealed that people in Merthyr Tydfil felt most 'poorly' with 18.1%. People in Blaenau scored 16.5%, Neath Port Talbot 16.4%, Rhondda 15.7% with only 15% of Caerphilly folk feeling 'under the weather'.

24. Ivor was a well-known singer on TV and radio.

25. Gryff Rhys Jones.

26. Pirate or buccaneer. However, after he had made his money at his chosen career he gave up piracy, became respectable and took a job with the government as Acting Governor of Jamaica.

27. 1997. The Welsh Highland Light Railway opened the first section of a public-service steam-hauled railway from Caernarfon to Dinas. Diesel-hauled out of the tourist season, the line will eventually link Caernarfon to Porthmadog and serve the local rural community as well as visitors to the area.

28. Painters.

29. St. David. It is not known exactly when he lived but it was around the 6th century. His first biography was not written until 1090 by Rhygyfarch, a bishop of St. David's.

30. The National Health Service. 'Nye' Bevan was the main architect of the NHS and used the principles on which the Tredegar Medical Aid Association had been built.

31. He sings. He's a top operatic bass-baritone.

32. Nicky Wire and James Bradfield of the Manic Street Preachers were first and third and were split by Kelly Jones of the Stereophonics in second place.

33. In a purpose-built coracle.

34. A Romantic Garden at their home Plas Newydd. Lady Eleanor Butler and the Honourable Sarah Ponsonby, known as the 'Ladies of Llangollen' lived in Plas Newydd in the 18th and early 19th centuries. They were visited by many famous and distinguished people of the time. The garden is now a well-known tourist attraction.

35. Be given to the Church. The animals were then either kept by the priest or vicar or sold back to the farmer to obtain income.

36. A language. It was the written form of an old Irish script which survived in Wales. Its meaning was only deciphered when stones with Ogam script and a Latin equivalent were found, and scholars were at last able to work out its meaning.

37. Welsh tea.

38. Because the rod shore-caught record for each of these fish is held from Welsh beaches.

39. A National Botanical Garden known as the Garden of Wales situated in the Tywi Valley between Swansea, Carmarthen and Llandeilo.

40. 67%, so answers of 57% and 67% will be OK.

41. Richard Burton. He was on his way up in Hollywood when he was Marcellus Gallio in 'The Robe' in '53, at the height of his fame as Mark Anthony in 'Cleopatra' in '63 and made his last appearance in Orwell's '1984' where the main character is taken to the torture room known as Room 101, from which the TV programme got its name.

42. Beer. Brains is Wales biggest independent brewer.

43. Tom Jones.

44. He was the first war correspondent onto the Normandy beaches.

45. The singer Dorothy Squires.

46. A windmill.

47. The Tories.

48. Butch Cassidy and the Sundance Kid. They were pursued over the Mexican border by Pinkertons around 1905 but got away

to Chile where they went on to Patagonia and joined the Welsh community who had settled there. It is said they lived among the Welsh community and bred horses.

49.   Shirley Bassey (christened Eliza Bassey) sang the Bond title songs for Goldfinger, Diamonds are Forever and Moonraker.

50.   Braveheart or William Wallace. William Wallace's name is said to have come from William Wallensis or William the Welshman because the Strathclyde Scots spoke a Welsh dialect until around the 12th century. Mel Gibson, though born in New York, grew up in Australia and played Wallace in the Hollywood film Braveheart.

51.   It was all reported on the Welsh American website and happened not so long ago in Southern California. Where else?

52.   Their Welsh family name. They changed their name to de la Pole.

53.   It means, 'In loving memory' and is found on tombstones all over Wales.

54.   Anglesey, Brecon, Caernarfon, Cardigan, Carmarthen, Denbigh, Flint, Glamorgan, Merioneth, Montgomery, Monmouth, Pembroke and Radnor. You can add the ending 'shire' to those where it fits, if you like.

55.   He was joint winner of the Nobel Prize. He got it for Physics.

56.   Roald Dahl.

57.   Football. He had a long and distinguished career for Manchester City and Wales and was the first footballer to be promoted in the modern way with endorsements etc.

58.   A house.

59. Hong Kong.

60. Whisky.

61. Write a poem. It is a big annual poetry competition.

62. Michael Howard.

63. A Camera Obscura.

64. Ivor Novello.

65. A spoon. Ornately carved 'love spoons' are a Welsh tradition, known now mostly through tourist sales. However, the symbols carved onto or around the handles of the spoon all have special meanings for those who can still interpret them.

66. On a wedding day. It was an old custom – still practised in some rural parts – for the bridegroom and his friends to come to 'kidnap' his bride from her family home and take her off to marry her. It was common for the bride to disguise herself when the groom and friends came to kidnap her from her fathers' house on the wedding day. The bride would often dress as an old lady knitting in the corner, or nursing a young baby boy (the young boy was a sign of good luck).

67. Cool Cymru. Whether this came before, after or at the same time as Cool Britannia I have no idea, but it sounds just as bad and died the death just as quickly when the hip young things moved on to the next big thing.

68. Road signs, as Wales uses both Welsh and English.

69. Natural lakes. It has around 400 natural lakes and around 90 reservoirs.

70. The garden sparrow, with the starling coming second and the blue-tit third.

71. The New Year. The Church changed to the Gregorian Calendar in 1752 and New Year moved to its present date.

72. Media. John was BBC Wales Arts and Media Correspondent at the time.

73. They wanted to change the name of part of North Parade and name it for Owain Glyndŵr. The Chamber of Commerce, for some reason, objected and a small revolution broke out.

74. Three; Cwm Deri Vineyard, Pembroke; Sugarloaf Vineyard, Abergavenny; and Worthenbury Vineyard, near Wrexham.

75. They were the first brewers in Europe (and maybe the world) to produce canned beer.

76. The Welsh version has more of the letter L. In fact it has 27 more.

77. Bertrand Russell.

78. Terry Jones, of Monty Python fame.

79. A car. Gilbern were set up by a Welsh master butcher **Gil**es Smith and a German engineer **Bern**ard Friese to build sports cars in the Rhondda in the 1950s.

80. None. It's a cheese-based sausage.

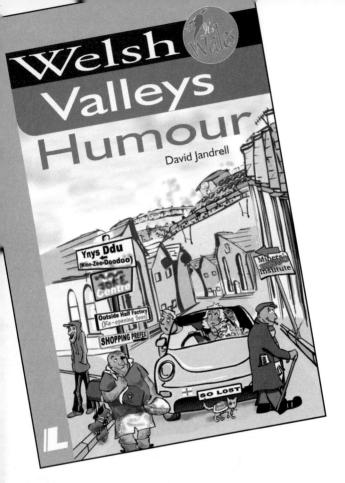

WELSH VALLEYS HUMOUR

David Jandrell

086243 736 9   £3.95

A tongue-in-cheek guide to Valleys English, with anecdotes and jokes.

"What a delight David Jandrell's book is!" *Ronnie Barker*

WELSH CHEESE RECIPES

Justin Rees

086243 721 0   £3.95

"Justin's colourful recipes are packed with taste and Welsh cheese is the best!" *Mike Doyle, Welsh TV Entertainer*

WELSH JOKES

Dilwyn Phillips

086243 619 2 £3.95

Meet the hymn-singing, beer-swilling, sheep loving true Welshman. This book contains the best, worst and dirtiest of Welsh jokes. Use on all occasions!

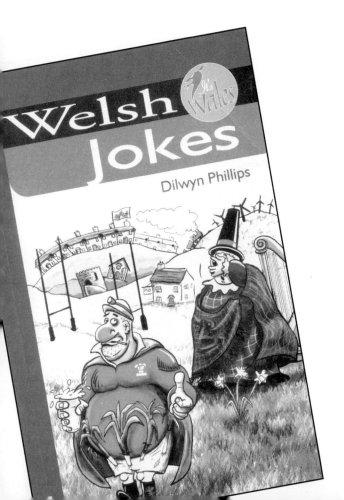

Already published

in the _It's Wales_ series:

More to follow!

The *It's Wales* series
is just one of a whole range
of Welsh-interest publications from Y Lolfa.
For a full list of books currently in print,
send now for your free copy
of our new, full-colour catalogue –
or simply surf into our website
www.ylolfa.com
for secure, on-line ordering.

Talybont, Ceredigion, Cymru SY24 5AP
e-bost ylolfa@ylolfa.com
gwefan www.ylolfa.com
ffôn (01970) 832 304
ffacs 832 782